TOBIAS

A CHEROKEE'S

SEARCH FOR

MANHOOD

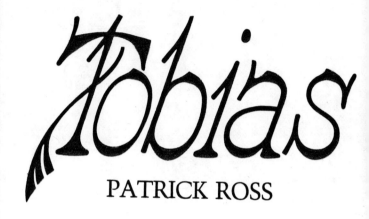

Tobias

PATRICK ROSS

**Tyndale House
Publishers, Inc.
Wheaton, Illinois**

Coverdale House
Publishers, Ltd.
Eastbourne, England

Original drawings
by Scott W. Brady.
Spanish translations
provided by Ernestina
Rodriguez Santos.

Library of Congress
Catalog Card Number
76-47280.
ISBN 0-8423-7250-4,
paper.
Copyright © 1976
by Tyndale House
Publishers, Inc.,
Wheaton, Illinois.
All rights reserved.
First printing,
February 1977.
Printed in the
United States of
America.

CONTENTS

FOREWORD

Tobias is only a story. Yet within its pages lies an accumulation of scenes, experiences, and feelings that are real enough to me. While my own search as a mixed-blood Cherokee happened under different circumstances and in a different time, I most surely have walked that same circle and felt the same depth of emotions as the youth in this narrative.

I am a daily observer of loncliness and hostility. My heart leaps out to those who now are where I once was before the solution came to me at last.

This book, then, provides what I have come to know is the only answer to the longings of those who seek love, truth, and real life.

Patrick Ross
July 1976

PREFACE   Motivated by
the Sequoyan
"alphabet," the entire Cherokee
nation became literate by 1830.
Young men and women studied in
Tsalagi seminaries and obtained
college degrees. And yet education
did not make them insensitive to
the simple beauty of Tsalagi
legends and myths. For centuries
these stories have maintained their
beauty and truth.

As a young boy I sat beneath the
pine and listened to the sound of
running water and the song of the
breeze. My great-grandfather
always said that their song was that
of Long Man, the Spirit of our
Provider. Listening to him and his
counsel of wisdom and experience,
I fell in love with the legends of our
people. My favorite is the story of
the pine, for within it I have seen
myself.

According to the Tsalagi, when
the world began, seven carefree and
careless boys wasted their thoughts
and time playing ball and dancing
rather than tending the cornfields
and hunting the squirrel as they had
been taught. Because the mothers

of these boys knew no way to make them change, they conspired to prepare their irresponsible sons a supper of steaming stones instead of the usual bean bread and rabbit. In outrage at what they considered an insult, these rebellious young men appealed to the spirits to sweep them far away from such harsh discipline.

Soon all seven boys began circling in the spinning feather dance. Faster and faster they whirled until the frenzied rebels were lifted slowly into the deepening blue. As the boys were lifted higher and higher, their frightened mothers rushed out to pull them back to earth. All of the women were too late except one, who with a long slender pole managed to reach up and pull her son down to the ground. But the boy fell so fast and struck the earth with such force that his body sank deep down into the soil and disappeared forever.

The remaining six boys continued to rise as their mothers wailed in distress from below. At length each of those six took his permanent place to form a small star constellation known to our people today as "The Boys."

All seven mothers were stricken with grief by the loss of their sons. But the mother of the boy who sank deep into the earth mourned with greater sorrow than any other. Each day she knelt beside his grave, weeping so long and hard that the earth always remained dampened by her tears. As days drew on and the tears of her care fell tenderly to the earth where her son had disappeared, a fresh sprout appeared and eventually grew into the tall and stately pine of today. My people believe that because of the pine's kinship to the stars, the beautiful tree holds within it the same infinite light as those heavenly bodies.

This legend of the pine is the story of that quest by seven headstrong and impetuous young boys who, like youth since the beginning of time, yearned for independence and freedom. In the struggle to have their own way, one of the seven remains today because he alone was forced to accept the love and concern of someone who cared. Through the tears of his mother, the dampened ground provided the fertile soil for his rebirth in the form of a young, delicate sprout. His continuing growth also remained dependent on her nurturing care. The legend of the pine illustrates that all who live, regardless of their strength and independence, require the love and concern of others.

The Indian continues to seek such wisdom in the creation which surrounds him. The stillness of the lakes, the gentle voice of running water, and the silence of the desert sands quietly touch his spirit and speak of truth.

His story and mine are the same; for I, Redbird, belong to the Real People.

Listen then as I share with you. Run with me through my experiences; walk with me through my dreams and visions; listen to Long Man in the sound of running water and the song of summer's breeze; and through it all taste, as I have, the bitterness of raw sap as well as the sweetness of the bee's honey. Then perhaps you, too, can understand their essence and choose between existence and real life.

I Will Lift My Eyes to the Hills

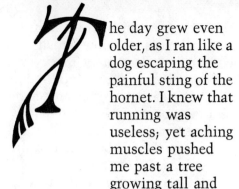he day grew even older, as I ran like a dog escaping the painful sting of the hornet. I knew that running was useless; yet aching muscles pushed me past a tree growing tall and proud beside the dirt trail, then beyond a crooked post stripped of its outer bark and laid bare to the ravages of woodworms, and finally toward a drooping weed leaning ragged and dusty.

As these distance markers blurred until nothing but shadows remained, I fell headfirst into the dirt road. On the worn rim of consciousness, I struggled to stand. In despair, I spit into the powdery dust of the sun-dried trail and wiped my mouth with the back of my hand. Too exhausted to run farther, I stumbled under that weight of bitterness and confusion to my only refuge, the river.

There above the water I stretched out on the leaning trunk of a flood-toppled cottonwood and thought about myself. I watched the still surface, below which churned a wild current that was never still and never quiet. Like the river, I was calm on the surface but churning beneath. I remembered Dad's saying once that still water runs deep. Then I became lost in the shadows above me.

My attention moved to one of nature's freaks on the low bank nearby. A towering pecan joined hands with a gentle water elm to form one giant timber. A rough, gnarled scar marked the union of the two trunks. I had often lost myself in the shadows of those leafy branches. As I lay there, my heart made its ancient and all too familiar plea, "Why isn't there someone?" How I longed for that bond of perfection that would see beyond all weaknesses, would listen with perception and compassion, and would speak with concern and wisdom.

But at fourteen I found little hope of discovering such an ideal. Dad was gone forever. Mom lay desperately ill in a tuberculosis sanitorium miles away. And I in my narrow cell of loneliness grew more bitter every day.

There on that cottonwood I angrily condemned my violent actions. I was certain that defending myself was justified, but I realized that people would only call it the Indian coming out in me. Fighting when you're a "half-breed" is barbaric and pagan. The facts plainly shouted that I had failed myself again.

As I lay suspended in time, the afternoon and the evening moved forward without me. The tirelessly flowing river, the cool, damp, woody smell of the bottomland, the strong, rough bodies of the pecans with their irregular webbing of leaves and branches overhead eventually calmed my anger. When day finally closed, I watched the drifting silhouette of a floating log cut the shimmering image of the moon on the surface of the river and send fleeting waves from each distorted part.

Straddling the tree, I stood to go as the strong and continuous glow of the full moon lighted my way to the shadowy bank. But then, with only steps to go, the moonlit night dimmed suddenly to the darkness of crude oil. Looking up, I saw that the smoky haze of a small, dark cloud covered the assuring brightness of the rising moon. However, in defiance of the night and its shadows, I blindly resumed my precarious and darkened pathway, groping with my left foot along the rough bark of the leaning tree. Suddenly a sharp pain cut into my foot and slashed up to my groin. Then as if pushed by some monstrous, invisible force, I fell from the rough tree into the dark water and plunged to the bottom. Although I tried to shove upward to free myself from the river's cold and murky depths, the fiery ache paralyzed me and left my body helpless. I was at the river's mercy as the swift current carried me in darkness. The river and the night seemed to flow into one eternal shadow. Above my fears, the untamed current roared a caution as it surged between the river's narrowing banks toward the old river bridge crouched somewhere ahead. Below its sagging timbers the water swirled ruthlessly. I was almost to the breaking point in this liquid race between death and darkness when my fears exploded into terror. Then the current shot me under the bridge, viciously slamming my body against the twisted roots and debris tangled around the heavy, rotting pilings. As throat and lungs screamed for air, I groped for some alternative to death. Finally a state of panic consumed all of my remaining strength, without which I could not reach light and life above.

My strength was gone. My life seemed lost to the ravenous current. But then, as if by a special miracle destined for that particular moment, I heard Dad's voice call clearly above the roar, "Now, Buckshot, if you ever get in a tight spot when you're swimming, just relax and let the water lift you to the surface like a green stick." Exhausted but hopeful, I ceased struggling and reached for the surface, which was bright now with the brilliance of the full moon in a cloudless sky.

As the water lifted me, I felt

life-giving air race into my aching lungs. My throat and nose burned with a sensitive reawakening to life. Then from within my quaking temples, the relentless pulse of my heart defied death.

A few seconds later, I slid to a stop on what felt like an island of solid rock. The merciful current had pushed me onto the safety of a tiny gravel bar that rose midstream from the depths of the rushing water. Safe at last on this tiny island, I breathed deep and sighed in relief.

Relief was short-lived, though, for almost immediately the searing pain returned as a reminder of the threat to my life. Exhausted from my struggle and numbed by the throbbing pain, I fell into depression and then shock.

In my condition time seemed not to pass. Breathing was difficult. It was as if the morning sun refused to rescue me with the light of day. The bright moon became a miniature rainbow with white shafts of light streaking downward from its center. Finally a cry began within me and escaped into the expanse of the night. "Please, God," I shouted, "send someone!" At that instant a flickering beam shone through the darkness to the right. Following that mysterious light, I managed strength to stand and shout a second time.

Then without knowing why or how, I ran harder and faster than ever before in my life. I knew that the fiend of my nightmares was chasing me and that no one would give me refuge. Instead only those solemn unspeaking faces stared with pity before hands slammed shut the massive wooden doors in my face. Darting into the shadows, I managed to lose him. But suddenly without warning, that fiendish, terrifying face appeared again, laughing insanely and shouting, "Your life is mine now or any time!"

Screaming a defiant "No!", I ran even harder and faster, searching desperately for escape. I was tired and afraid, but no one came. My heart pounded until it burst with an explosion of paralyzing fear. I turned quickly to face him and thrust open my eyes. Before me was the quiet reassurance of Uncle Jim's smiling face. Dazed and utterly confused, I sighed in relief, realizing that I was alive and somewhere, anywhere, but not in that cold, dark river.

Three days later I regained my strength and was able to return to fresh air and sunshine. I was thankful, for I hated the confining walls of the hospital. Driving with Uncle Jim to the big white farmhouse, I hoped that somehow my life there would be different. But as I stepped from the warm sunlight into the cool shade of the front porch, Aunt Liz swung open the front door and snapped, "Tobias, wipe your feet before you come into my house!" They were the same condescending words that had issued her "welcome" when I had first come to live with Uncle Jim. Yet her command was more than an immaculate housewife wanting a young boy to clean his feet before walking across varnished floors.

To Aunt Liz, my Indian father was a disgrace to the family, and his half-breed son was a continued reminder of her humiliation. Consequently, she never missed a chance to remind me that I was inferior to her and needed to improve myself in order to live under her roof. Furthermore, she refused me the right to talk of my heritage to anyone. Of course, everybody knew that Dad was Cherokee; so I laughed at Aunt Liz's demand that I hide the fact that I was half.

But at fourteen this laughter trembled as I became the object of humiliation when Aunt Liz forbade me to include my Cherokee ancestry in a seventh grade history class heritage report. At first I was stunned. I could not believe that she would deny me the right to acknowledge my background. Yet Aunt Liz made this demand as if she could control my life, and to my dismay she almost did. A quick phone call to my history teacher insured that I would not be required to read my report aloud.

On the day the assignment was due, I seethed within while quietly listening to each of my classmates read proudly about his heritage. Finally, when only I had remained silent, a taunt rose from the back of the room, "What's wrong, Tobias? Ashamed to tell us about your Indians?" Of course, this mockery came from a boy who did not know whether his people had come from Ireland, Germany, or Timbuktu. Filled with rage, I rose from my seat and wheeled to face him. Grabbing his skinny, grimy neck, I squeezed until the jeer left his eyes and the smirk fled his pale face. Finally, when I realized my anger, saw his fear, and heard his choking gasps, I dropped him, whining like a scolded pup, onto the floor. Only then, trembling in the calm of my anger, did I hear the teacher's frightened shouts as I turned slowly to meet the fear and disappointment within her expression.

From that day at school I was labeled a troublemaker. School then became a prison of public humiliation in partnership with the private humiliation at the place I was forced to call home. With the words, "Tobias, wipe your feet before you come into my house" echoing in my mind, I considered how foolish I had been to think that my situation would be different. Again and again those words lashed the back of my self-respect while mocking my lonely and silent cry for someone who cared.

And so without that someone or even the pretense of a loving family, the river became the core of my existence. My fascination for the potential power of the unharnessed stream never ceased. Consequently, the little river framed with luxuriant masses of emerald ferns and water grasses provided a sanctuary from the critical attacks of school and home.

Standing beneath the rough-barked pecans and walnuts, the strong and towering oaks and cypress, I calmed to the gentle song of nature. Gurgling water accompanied the raucous chorus of bugs rehearsing audio exercises within the leafy canopy of mustang grapes that crept up and across the tender crowns of the smaller trees. The peace and beauty of this natural scene was my warm blanket against the chilling rejection of the all-white community.

But there were times when the natural beauty of the river was not enough to give refuge. When the warm, quiet afternoons and evenings became endless, life in a home where I was unwelcome became unbearable. Aunt Liz's "Wipe your feet, Tobias!" emphasized her resentment, and Uncle Jim's never failing comment, "Mind your Aunt Liz" bound the two of them in a position of dutiful sacrifice. In their home I was alone.

The loneliness cut so deeply that not even the river erased its pain. Again and again I wondered why there was not a person in the whole world who really cared enough to listen to me. Then I would recall Dad's strength, his wisdom, his concern and understanding, and wish once more for his protective, unselfish love.

Uncle Jim and Aunt Liz gave me a place to stay, but I resented having to live with them in their big, empty house where love and compassion were strangers. There, only social grace and Christian "duty" seemed welcome. But a mile away, if I climbed through the fence and crossed the pasture, there was a real home with an atmosphere like ours had been before Dad was killed and Mom got sick. Carmen and Antonio's family lived there on their small five acres of family happiness. Their home, like the river, was my place of refuge. Their father, a strong and smiling man whose favorite expression was "No work, no eat," was tractor foreman for a large farm. His two middle children, Antonio and Carmen, were my only friends. I enjoyed being with them and their family, and often tramped over to their home. Its atmosphere was like the serenity of my river. And whenever the river's peaceful flow could not offer refuge, their simple home did. Content with life, appreciative of each other, tolerant of strangers, these people possessed a way of life I longed to share.

Antonio's mother's smile was filled with the warm love that only a mother has for her son. And no matter how busy, she always offered me some of her delicious beans rolled in a soft flour tortilla. At Christmas and Easter, she sent me tamales, hot with pepper and tasting like my grandmother's bean bread. My appreciation for this family increased and so did my visits to their home.

Uncle Jim knew about my visits, and also he knew how much Aunt Liz disapproved. To her, being of their race was lower than being Indian. "Put that long sleeved shirt on and wear your hat, Tobias!" she demanded, unable to bear the thought of my being as "dark as those children." And so, rebelliously I did all I could to stay tanned as old leather, even going without a shirt on warm winter days.

Then Antonio hired out to Uncle Jim on Saturdays and after school. As the two of us worked together, he taught me Spanish. This really infuriated Aunt Liz. With great pride she always boasted of her family's giving up their language after migrating from the "old country." Aunt Liz's intolerance of a person's stubborn refusal to relinquish his native tongue was obvious when she proudly boasted, "If we could do it, so can they." At that time I was too young to see that her background made it impossible to understand the reasons one culture gives up its language or any other tradition while another clings tenaciously.

Ironically Antonio's dad once referred to some white people as not being "so good as the other white people." He concluded that this must have been so because of the hatred and contempt with which they had been treated during both world wars. I felt strong resentment against Aunt Liz's attitude toward anything not lily white. However, around her friends I practiced my own deceit by becoming a polite stoic. I hated their fabricated smiles and pretended concern, and day by day the psychological chasm that isolated me from any real beauty or happiness widened. These friends loyally supported Aunt Liz and counseled me "not to pal around with *those* people."

Their good intentions, however, brought no results. Eventually Aunt Liz went so far as to forbid me to sit with my friends on the school bus. With this, she pushed too hard, and obstinately I made certain that I sat with Antonio and Carmen every day. However, through the tattling mouths of my classmates, Aunt Liz learned of my continued and deliberate disobedience. To punish me, she threatened to take away certain privileges. I remember laughing cynically as I wondered, "What privileges?"

In the course of events that had followed my fight the day of my near drowning, Aunt Liz eventually demanded an explanation. When I refused, she ordered Uncle Jim to punish me for what she called my "disgracefully uncivilized behavior!" In spite of her orders, Uncle Jim did nothing more than dutifully send me to my room.

Sprawled across my bed, I recalled the circumstances that had provoked my anger on that day. It was the final day of the school year. The afternoon was hot as we rode the bus home from school. Carmen, Antonio, and I sat in our usual places about four seats from the rear of the bus. Oblivious of everyone, we laughed in sheer joy that school was closing for the year and discussed plans for a summer of change. Suddenly that first paper airplane sailed past my right shoulder and crashed rudely into the seat-back before us. Ignoring its hateful intent, we continued talking; however, when the second missile jabbed my neck, every seething emotion and muscle within me tensed until I became a coiled rattlesnake silently waiting for the slightest provocation. Then every atom in me split as a crude note, deliberately designed to make me strike, slid swiftly past my burning ear and landed ungracefully in Carmen's lap. Its repulsive message, "Half-breed + Meskin = red dirt," cut painfully into my grain. I whirled to face three white-trash albinos grinning like crooked-toothed lizards on the back seat of the bus. Just then the packed school bus jerked to an unexpected halt. With gritted teeth and clenched fists, I sprang vindictively toward the oldest boy and shoved him roughly through the emergency exit.

Following like a whirlwind, I leaped on him, viciously slamming his shaggy blonde head against the solid surface of the gravel road until shrill screams of the frightened girls and angry shouts of the bus driver jolted me back to reality. That skimmed milk face had colored to a sweating, dingy red as I squeezed his skinny throat until his pale eyes bulged. Resisting a final impulse to smash his pimply nose, I let go of his trembling form, left him lying there panting in the dirt, and ran. It was after this that I had come close to drowning in the dark, swift water.

Reminded of the river, I decided to go there. So slipping out quietly, I left by the back door and headed toward the refreshing coolness of my river.

The warm sun said good morning to my shirtless back, and my bare feet passed on the same friendly greeting to the earth below. Absorbed by the warmth of the morning sun, the feel and smell of the plowed earth, the damp freshness of the open air, I soon reached the vibrant stream, stood still, and listened. The summer breeze whispered through the leaves as finches and redbirds whistled confidently above the soft voice of the flowing, reassuring river.

Renewed by its song, I climbed out onto my strong cottonwood. After first making certain that no poisonous scorpion lurked there, I again straddled its huge trunk confidently and allowed the cold water to clean the dust from my dangling feet. Above the river a translucent blue sky condensed into cotton fluffs which passed over only to dissipate into the boundlessness of heaven. Upriver, tiny stars of sunlight trod lightly upon the shining current. Looking downstream, I smiled at the sight of the old bridge hunched feebly now in the light between its supporting banks. Every rotten plank and rail hung so worn and weak that a butterfly's breath alone could cause it to collapse. There it lay at the mercy of all who crossed, while the ageless river flowed smoothly on.

In those surroundings I communed with the quiet spirit of my natural sanctuary as my embittered mind and body relaxed in the freedom of nature. There I was courteously received, with the one condition that I accept and respect everything with reverent appreciation, understanding, and tolerance.

Dad had first taught me this lesson in the art of coexistence—to sit very patiently and quietly while listening, watching, and sensing the importance of each small part of nature, regardless of how unimportant it seemed. Through sensitivity I learned to walk without trampling or disturbing; to hunt and fish without senseless greed or sadistic pleasure; to hear and see beauty within simplicity; and to sense the great span between freedom and captivity, life and mere existence.

I learned that nature is without a

doubt one of this world's greatest teachers. In her classroom, my boy's inquisitive mind grew into acute curiosity. In amazement I watched wood ants traverse their worn and narrowly distinct little trails, carrying on their individual backs bits of leaves three times the size of their bodies. I listened with awe to the loud summer song of the happy cricket whose only vocal cords were two tiny hind legs.

Perched lazily upon my low water bridge, I pondered the nearby mystery of that freak fusion between the two specied trees into the expanse and growth of a single huge timber with towering branches leafed either as elm or pecan. Raw sap oozed from the gnarled scar which marked the natural and yet freakish graft of the two trees. My curiosity unsatisfied, I felt compelled to do more than merely view the scene. Carefully returning to the bank, I climbed the base of the elm to the scar and with forefinger traced the sticky juice to a small knothole. My imagination pictured a cavern of golden sweet honey; but expectantly licking the thick, sticky liquid from my finger, I tasted sharply the disappointing bitterness of raw sap. This shock to my taste buds, however, evidently relayed a message to my stomach; and with the vascillating curiosity of a young boy, I immediately began to speculate upon what might be for dinner that day.

Making my way back through the river bottom and up the shady road, I recalled Uncle Jim's warning me to forget my bitterness and become a man like Dad. This advice only served to intensify my resentment, for I was certain that without Dad for an example, I could never learn the secret of his maturity and strength. Useless to me, it lay isolated with his family over 300 miles away in East Texas.

So many answers were there, including the solution to who I really was as a Tsalagi. Because this Indian heritage dominated my life as naturally as red paint stands out on a white wall, my identification with it seemed crucial. Dad had taught me to have pride in being Indian. But he had not had time to tell me why. I yearned for the real story of the Indian, and especially the Tsalagi. I thought that if I knew the facts about the past as well as the present, I could stand tall as a young Tsalagi. In Pine Tree I could learn to respect myself and consequently have an inner strength with which to face intolerance, misunderstanding, and prejudice. And above all, in spite of the staggering weight of those destructive three, I could find a way to be accepted for what I really was: a mixed-blood Indian sitting precariously upon the solid wall separating the white world from the red. For these reasons, unconscious as they were then, I longed desperately for a life with my grandparents. As a child of that day but as a man for the future, I knew that somehow there had to be a better way.

However, I feared that Aunt Liz would soon destroy my dream of going to East Texas. The helplessness experienced in my nightmares settled upon me like an oppressive cloud as I recalled the hateful prophecy of my dreamworld assailant—"your death will be slow and horrible!" However, before the frightening words engulfed me in total depression, the stillness of the warm air seemed to voice Dad's familiar philosophy on dreams— "Buckshot, nothing is impossible until you have tried. Look at the bumblebee. Scientists say it is impossible for him to fly; but he doesn't know it, so he flies."

By the time I had walked the mile and a half to the farmhouse, Dad's advice had crystallized into a determined faith that this dream of mine would become a reality. I was going to Pine Tree. I could pack my stuff after Uncle Jim and Aunt Liz had gone to bed and then slip away early the next morning before they awoke.

That night at supper Uncle Jim looked unusually tired and worried. However, my selfish determination forced my attention from him as I filled my plate. From the stacked platter of crisp-fried chicken I took a thick, crusty drumstick and breast, then heaped half my plate with potatoes. After mashing them with lots of thick cream gravy, I spooned fresh pinto beans onto my crowded plate. Then on top of everything, I piled several thick slices of home-grown tomatoes and fresh-chilled cucumbers.

But when I glanced back in Uncle Jim's direction, his solemn eyes spoke of fatigue and sadness. He pushed away from the table and mumbled, "Tobias, come outside with me. We need to talk."

As I followed him from the kitchen and out into the quiet stillness of the warm night, I saw the moon in its final quarter hanging ominously like a luminous sickle against the darkness of the summer sky. Uncle Jim stood, hands thrust deep into his khaki pockets, and faced the bright glow of Venus. Then turning to me, he spoke in a strained, broken voice. "They just called from the tuberculosis sanitorium, Toby. Your mother is gone. I'm sorry. God rest her soul. She was the only one I had left."

We just stood staring into each

other's hearts. I was stunned. I couldn't believe she was really gone. I couldn't speak, and it seemed that Uncle Jim couldn't either. Suddenly he looked down at the ground, and I could then see his shoulders silently crumbling from their manly height. As he shook with grief, too proud to cry, I realized how special Mom had been to him. He turned and walked slowly through the shadows and toward the house. He glanced back for an instant, then hurried through the door and faded into the darkness. The thump of the front screen punctuated the silence and concluded all beginnings. Suddenly, one at a time, Dad and Mom had disappeared from my life, just as Uncle Jim had vanished into the dark stillness of his big white house.

Numbed and confused, I walked away and into the grassy yard. I wanted to cry but could not find the gentle sensitivity which triggers tears. Sinking to my knees and rolling over on my back, I gazed solemnly into the clear summer night as I longed for one last moment with Mom. The crescent moon seemed superimposed with the bright beams of a glowing cross. Wiping away the tears and glancing away, I stared into the night, then moments later caught sight of an almost naked figure with outstretched arms urging me to come along. Sensing the need to go, I was spirited to his place, high in the sky, and the two of us became one. His smile was warm.

Then together we turned to climb the soaring beams. As a solitary figure, we rose higher and higher to plateaus of brilliant height. As we moved outward to what seemed like the edge of eternity, I grew afraid, then separated and slid away and apart from him, no longer absorbed by the now-glowing figure who stepped off into everything. After a wide-eyed glimpse, a colorless blink and nothing more, I slipped off into a crimson, striated sky.

The sharp bark of the collie pup at my side jolted me back to reality, where I stared wonderingly beyond the slate suede sky into the twinkling face of a summer star.

Alone and confused, I clenched my fists and shouted, "Why? Why me?"

Shackled by self-pity, as I hobbled within a narrow cell of bitterness, I resented the events surrounding Mom's burial. The beautiful flowers and tears reeked with hypocrisy, for I knew how critical everyone must have been of Mom's marriage to Dad. Somehow I never believed that they had really been accepted as man and wife. And because everybody rejected that union, they also rejected me. I hated them for it.

The day after the funeral, I told Uncle Jim that I was leaving for Pine Tree. He didn't seem surprised. "Toby," he said, "your dad dreamed of the day he could finally take you to his people, but your mother feared that you would prefer their way of life."

Uncle Jim drove me to the bus station the next morning. At the Old City Hotel where the bus depot was located, he paid the fare. When I had unloaded my suitcases, I sat on the curb to wait. The sky seemed to forecast a cloudy day. Handing me my ticket, Uncle Jim explained that the bus would come along in a couple of hours. As he turned to leave, his voice seemed sincere. "Give them my best regards. They are fine people, Toby—and friends." Before I had time to respond, he climbed into his pickup and drove away. Those two thoughts!—"fine people" and "friends"—wrestled for my attention as I stood staring across the highway at the railroad tracks. Suddenly I bitterly recognized the hypocrisy in both expressions. Uncle Jim was as gutless as Aunt Liz. If he had really felt that my grandparents were fine people and friends, he had completely sidestepped these facts in order to avoid friction and community ridicule.

I was too angry to sit. Taking my gear, I raced across the highway, daring an oncoming trailer truck. Then the tables turned, and I was challenged by a stubborn iron engine blocking my path. To run any farther, I would either have to go over, under, or around this standing hulk of power and its trailing wheels of freight. I stood staring at three flatcars loaded with cedar posts as my anger smoldered to depression. Kicking rocks along the tracks and watching them scatter, I heard a cheerful voice call, "Don't you worry, son; you won't have to dig post holes for all those cedars." I turned to meet the smiling, round face of an engineer leaning from his window. Grinning broadly, he advised, "Better get along now, young fellow; this train is leaving in ten minutes, and I don't want you under the wheels."

With a solemn "Yes, sir!" I moved reluctantly down the tracks in the direction of the bus station, thinking that it might just be my luck for that bus never to arrive. Then, watching a bee dart among the blossoms of a crepe myrtle, I stood there in that loose gravel and made an impetuous decision. Within an instant I had decided to forget that Greyhound and instead hitch a free ride on the freight. I had heard Uncle Jim arrange with the ticket seller to keep an eye on me. She agreed to call them collect after I had safely boarded the right bus. I laughed contemptuously as I imagined Aunt Liz turning social cartwheels as she tried to mask her anger and humiliation with sincere concern for my safety.

To make sure that I was not being watched, I climbed between two of the cars, then jumped to the ground on the other side of the freight. I trotted down the tracks past a long line of refrigerated boxcars before seeing what I thought had to be the answer to some silent, unknown prayer. Stretching down the remainder of the tracks to the caboose stood a series of flatcars loaded with shiny new automobiles of every style and color imaginable. Each one seemed to be standing, waiting for me to open its door and climb inside.

Cautiously I scanned the track from engine to caboose but saw no one. Silencing a loud victory yell, I tossed up my suitcase and Dad's small awol bag before I scrambled up and into the front seat of the beautiful red convertible. Knowing that I must not be seen, I stretched out on the plush red leather. Then everything under me suddenly shifted with the unmistakable sound of railroad cars jolting forward.

As the iron wheels rolled faster, I confidently faced a clouded, blue sky. Town was behind me, and my pride swelled until it finally exploded into a war whoop that rang with triumph. Victory tasted sweet as I settled behind the wheel. Unzipping my bag, I dug to the bottom and pulled out a large apple I'd saved for lunch. Polishing it with my shirttail 'til I could see myself in its shiny red, I then enjoyed its delicious taste. The apple reminded me of Dad, for he liked apples more than any other fruit.

Memories of him moved into my thoughts. I recalled how war had come and separated us forever. He had left our family, our home, and his life. Then, just before Christmas after going overseas, he was killed. An attempt to halt an act of "unprovoked aggression" halfway around the world for people I didn't know had brought a full-scale war of my own into reality.

Mom had cried when news of Dad's death came and for a long

while after; but with time her crying eventually ceased. I never cried, never talked about him, but never forgot the happiness and security life held before he died. For us the simple ways had been our joy. During watermelon season we bought the big forty- and fifty-pound red-meated melons from the growers who trucked them into town in their sagging trucks. We chilled them between the moss-covered rocks in the cold, shallow river. Then, slicing into them with our pocket knives, Dad and I ate out their sweet, juicy hearts and left the seedy pulp and rinds for the cattle.

Sometimes while he worked at mending broken fences or trimming brush, I swung from low hanging grapevines. Then I'd stop to hold the fence stretcher while Dad hammered shiny staples into new cedar posts. I'd watch him bend the barbed wire back and forth to break it; but when I tried, the sharp barbs stuck and cut.

When work was done, we polefished with earthworms for Rio Grande perch. Baiting our trotlines with them, we tried for sleek catfish with sharp fins, broad flat heads, and catlike whiskers that threaded out from each corner of their wide frowning mouths.

If we didn't have time to sct out long trotlines from bank to bank, we used shorter throw lines. First, Dad decided on a good place to fish. Then he tied the ends of the heavy twisted lines to limber pecan seedlings or willows growing down close to the water's edge. They gave our catches enough play so that the hooks wouldn't pull out or the lines break before we could land them. After baiting each hook, sometimes using Crystal White soap squares if the water was muddy, Dad would grip the twelve to fourteen feet of line in two places. Then looking back at me, regardless of how far away or clear I stood, he yelled, "Now get back, Buckshot, so these hooks won't get you!" With that he would swing the rock-weighted end back a time or two and let go. Making a quiet splash, the line always fell just as Dad intended.

Life with Dad had been filled with good times, respect, and love. I sighed in relief that at last I was on my way to discovering the secret of his strength and patience. I wished I could snap my fingers to advance time and space and be there in Pine Tree. I figured I'd get off the train somewhere, anywhere, and then catch a bus the rest of the way.

Again I opened the old awol bag, and this time withdrew Dad's Bible. Uncle Jim had sent it along for Grandmother, "if," as he said, "you don't want it yourself, Toby." Opening its scuffed cover, I saw his name written in his strong, bold hand that curved and peaked with beauty. Below his name was scribbled a single page number. Wondering at its significance, I located the page in the Book of Psalms. I began to read, but before I had finished less than half a page, my concentration was spoiled by vaguely written thoughts about looking at the hills. Having lost interest, I closed the Bible, then held it above me, allowing the pages to come together at the center. As each page fell limply into place, I realized that the leaves had been shuffled many times. It was just like Dad to use something until it reflected his personality.

I recalled his pointing to row after row of fine new boots standing like soldiers at inspection, all spit-polished and identical on their shelves. As we had sauntered out of the stores and down the streets together, he smiled and whispered, "Look, Buckshot, how each man wears himself into his shoes." Dad wore himself into everything he owned until his possessions became just as I wanted to be. As I rode the train toward Pine Tree, memories of Dad were so real that they clouded all happiness and left me lonely and sad.

I stared at a chrome handle gleaming brilliantly in the white morning rays of the hot Texas sun and then away to the passing fields. In bitterness I wanted to race swiftly through the summer pastures of Johnson grass, standing parched, withered, and useless in the blazing sun. Their spring freshness had grown tough and burnt. Emerald sprouts no longer danced in and out among the primroses and wild verbena.

Defeated by the change in seasons, they were shriveled and inadequate to shade the tiny ground creatures from the wrath of the fiery sky. Where bluebonnet fields had once bloomed, only tall, rough-stalked sunflowers and prickly cockleburs stood as silent sentinels.

In spirit I longed to cross that dry prairie and then sink exhausted to my knees on the peaceful bank of a reinless river. There my mind—awhirl with its struggling, fighting thoughts—might be set free.

As quickly as it had begun, my free train ride braked to an unexpected halt. As I started to climb down, I heard someone crunch through the dry gravel beside the track. The certainty that he was searching for me and my fear of being discovered rolled me to the floorboard of my car. Lying there, sweat pouring from my rigid body, hot salt burning my face and neck, I became so intimidated by every sound that even my breathing seemed deliberate and voluntary. Fear had changed me into a frightened, cowering child, and I was ashamed.

I felt as if I were somewhere else, a solitary spectator viewing the total humiliating scene. Cursing my actions, defiantly I vowed never again to tremble in fear. As the trainman approached and passed on, I breathed deeply and relaxed. Then to regain self-respect, I grabbed my gear and proudly leaped from the flatcar. Holding my head high, I forced myself straight ahead. By the time I reached the highway I was thirsty, and quenching that thirst was uppermost in my mind. I crossed the highway, raced up concrete steps to a large old country store, pushed against the door bar, and entered through swinging screens. I reached into the icy water in a red cooler, pulled out a cream soda, and then enjoyed a long, cold swig. A large clock on the store wall warned me, though, that I had little time to spare; but with luck I could get back to catch that morning bus on time. I paid the grocer, dropped the empty bottle into a wooden case, and hurried out the door.

Standing on the concrete porch of the store, I spotted an old Chevy parked on the other side of the two-lane highway. An aged couple was trying to remove their spare from the car's trunk. Traffic was heavy; and as car after car sped past without stopping to offer help, I became annoyed at the condescending indifference of passersby. The root of their neglect appeared to me to be more than selfish preoccupation. It seemed a deliberate action to degrade and humiliate these people.

Finally, wind from a speeding vehicle rippled the old couple's clothing and sent the old man's straw hat toppling into the ditch. Reacting with hostility, I sprang to the asphalt below, picked up a broken brick, and hurled it behind the fading insult; then in contempt I kicked a beer can, sending it clattering end over end across the pavement.

In the heat of my anger I almost forgot my intentions to help the old couple. I quickly crossed the road and retrieved the old fellow's hat. Handing it to him I smiled and asked, *"Buenos diás. Le puedo ayudar con la llanta?"*

His dark eyes sparkling, he nodded. *"Si, si, puedes ayudarme. Necesito ayuda."*

Returning his smile and pointing toward the shade of a broadleafed post oak beside the road, I suggested, *"Vote a sentar te debajo del árbol. Yo le cambio la llanta."*

Nodding gratefully and saying, *"Gracias, gracias,"* they moved beneath the protective shade of the large tree.

Since the right rear tire was completely flat, sliding the jack under the low axle was not easy, especially on the grassy incline. After loosening the five lugs, I jacked up the car, then removed the ragged tire. After I replaced it with a worn spare, I gave each lug an extra turn, then kicked the hub cap in place. Rolling the flat around to the rear of the car, I heaved it and the tools into the trunk, slammed it shut, then called to the old couple, *"Vente ya ta compuesta la llanta."*

"Quisiera ofrecerte algo."

I was surprised that he thought I wanted pay. Sensing their embarrassment, I quickly replied, *"Oh, no quiero dinero, señor."*

As he said, *"Si un dia necesitas ayuda. Nosotros te podemos ayudar,"* I knew I had made a friend. Although my determination not to trust anyone was still fresh, I relaxed in the comfort and security of their companionship. Betraying caution and reason, I accepted their warmth and appreciation as sincere expressions of gratitude. Offering my hand, I introduced myself. The old man shook his head and asked, *"Ah! Yo creía que eras Mexicano!"*

Not surprised, yet proud that he had mistaken me for Mexican, I answered, *"No, soy Indio."*

"Ah!" he smiled and offered, *"Qué 'tas haciendo aquí, tan lejos de tu tierra?"*

I explained that I was not going home, but instead was headed west to catch an eastbound bus. Immediately he insisted, *"Ven con nosotros vamos pa quel rumbo. Nosotros te llevamos: tu nos ayudates, hora nos toca ayudarte."*

Accepting his offer, I replied,

"Gracias. Tengo gusto d'ir con gente buena."

He smiled and introduced first his wife and then himself as Señora and Señor Gonzales. Cheerfully she waved me toward the front seat of their car, then graciously settled her plump self in the back. Although she remained absolutely silent, her eyes seemed to whisper, "I care."

As we rode, I disclosed to them my plans for the summer. Smiling in sympathetic understanding, Señor Gonzales then revealed his recollection of some boyhood summer of his own. Señora Gonzales remained warmly alert and nodded pleasantly.

Miles vanished; then we were parked before the hotel bus stop, just as Uncle Jim and I had been earlier that morning. To complete the thank you's and good-bye's, Señora Gonzales touched my hand lightly and spoke for the first and only time. *"Que vayas con dios, Toby."* Behind her soft and sincere words echoed the groan of the Greyhound bus as it pulled into the station.

Looking back at Señor and Señora Gonzales for the last time, I waved. Such kind and gentle people, I thought. Soon I would learn this same truth about my own people in Pine Tree.

My shining coach to freedom and acceptance finally roared into the Greyhound depot at Pine Tree that summer day. My heart raced like a redbird's I once caught so cruelly in my homemade snare. My hands had cradled him ever so gently, yet he had shuddered in total mistrust. That day at the depot I shared the bird's fear of an unknown giant. Like that frightened bird, I wanted to fly far from my prison to escape the giants, loneliness and fear, and to soar high above insecurity and doubt, to find peace and freedom in the sunbathed treetops of my dreams.

But then searching the restless and impatient crowd, I could see no one looking for me. Disappointment laughed at my immature faith that my grandparents had received the telegram with the time of my arrival. Then humiliation and insecurity took the stand to criticize my foolish hope that I could escape unhappiness as the migrating cardinal flees the harshness of winter. I had hoped to fly from the chill winds of prejudice and loneliness to a land of eternal springtime warmed by hope and showered with love that would nourish a freshness into the drought of my life. Just like that redbird, I was a creature of nature, wild and untamed, and fiercely responsive to the struggle for survival. But as a human being, mere survival was not enough for me. Inside me, bitterness raged like an ice storm.

Moving with a deliberate determination to change the climate of my life, I stepped off that eastbound bus trying desperately to convince myself that having no one to meet me really didn't matter. After all, I had not come in search of someone to coddle me or cater to my emotional whims, but instead I had come to learn about my people. Yet staring at the blue and white bus as its powerful engine propelled it off down the smooth highway, I wondered if I would ever find home.

Again I searched the dispersing crowd of waiting people for my grandparents. Just when I had decided to ask for information, I noticed a tall, dark-skinned man in Levis and a khaki shirt watching me. He stared with discernment. Then with a voice as penetrating as his eyes, he questioned, "Tobias?"

"Yes, sir!" I responded automatically and in my deepest tones. The resonant challenge of his small, dark eyes faded into warm rays of sunlight that streamed in to rekindle the fire of my faded hope. Their message spoke clearly that I was welcome. I smiled within, for once again I saw Dad and knew that this dark man was not a stranger, but my grandfather.

At Dad's funeral I had had my first brief glimpse of him. He and Grandmother had sat behind us. Later he shook my hand, and she kissed me. But before they could come into my life, they had gone. Really seeing him for the first time, I sensed his quiet strength and pride. Lean muscles like those of a quarter horse and hair as jet as an angus denied his age. His heavy leather work boots, smooth and slick like the oil-soaked earth of Gregg County, spoke of his work in those famous East Texas fields.

Turning, he motioned to a small plump woman saying, "Mama, this is him." The contrasting dominance of her cheekbones and gentle eyes underlined her strong, yet delicate, beauty. Her raven hair was neatly spiraled in Tsalagi tradition into a smooth bun atop her proud head. Her clear, olive skin joined it in complementary perfection. As she kissed me, her dark moist eyes smiled. Then she spoke the most beautiful words I had ever heard. "Let's go home, Tobias."

The view from Agidutsi's pickup as we drove home was one of pine forests trailed with narrow oil-saturated dirt roads. The slash, loblolly, and shortleaf pine trees thrived side by side with scatterings of red oak, sweet gum, white oak, and wild maple. The timber was so thick that trees more than thirty yards into its denseness faded into a blur of almost total darkness.

As I stood beneath a large slash pine, I was relieved that Agilisi and Agidutsi had stepped into the lighted house and left me alone to watch and listen. Spears of brilliance hurled by the slowly setting sun cut the dense growth of tall pines and pierced their lengthening shadows below. These radiant shafts illumined and defined the heart of the scene and promised for another day a glimpse of what lay sleeping in the shade today. To accompany the contrasts of dancing light, the silent movement of the east wind breathed a tranquil music through the needled leaves like that of the river as it christened the small flat stones flung out in its path. Not only was I at home, but I also had a replacement for my river.

Assured by the memory of flowing water and stilled by the quiescent whistle of the pointed pines, I sensed also that I was no longer alone. Silently the strong, inspiring surroundings signed and sealed an intuitive, compelling covenant between myself and some infinite unknown.

Except for the tall slash pine branching above me, my grandparents' small company house rested alone in a small clearing surrounded by a dense growth of pines. I circled the outside of the tin-roofed, wood-framed construction; then, stooping to rake away the rusty pine needles, I scooped up a handful of red, sandy soil. As the summery earth slowly trickled from my upturned palm, I solemnly considered time.

Returning to the lone pine, I faced the house, then sauntered over to the front porch where I curiously peered through the darkness to glimpse what lay beneath. Some old ragged onions bunched with twine hung limply from the floor joists. Disappointed at finding nothing more interesting, I stood, dusted my knees, and somewhat reluctantly climbed the rough wooden steps. I knocked on the screen door, then heard a strong voice answer from somewhere

within, "Come in, Tobias."
Strengthened by the gentle whisper
of the pines, I opened the door and
stepped into the brightness of the
small front room.

Walking through to the kitchen, I
saw a vase of freshly cut roses on
the kitchen table. Behind them
stood Agilisi at the sink. On either
side of her were plank shelves lined
with jars of herbs and spices. To the
left of the cabinets stood the icebox
and stove, and to the right hung a
large wooden plaque. Hand-carved
letters boldly proclaimed:

I lift up my eyes to the hills.
From whence does my help come?
My help comes from the Lord,
who made heaven and earth.

Staring at this message, I recalled
the marked passage in Dad's Bible. I
would give it to Agilisi, for I could
not trust the words within its
pages. Looking back at her, I met
the warmth of her dark, smiling
eyes. "Supper is just about ready,"
she said as she dried her delicate
hands with her starched apron.

Then smoothing the wrinkles from the simple print, she explained that we would eat as soon as Agidutsi finished milking. Motioning for me to follow, Agilisi walked onto a narrow, screened shed room extending across the back side of the house. At one end stood a small metal cot covered with fresh, clean sheets. Neatly folded at its head lay a red plaid blanket with a small pillow resting on top. From the exposed rafters, a broom handle hung suspended on coat hanger wire. This was my closet. A homemade bootjack sat on the floor beside the bed, and a number three washtub for me to bathe in was pushed into the corner. As we turned to go, Agilisi added, "This room and everything in it was your father's, and now it is all yours."

I heard her words, but my eyes were fixed upon an empty white quiver hanging regally above the doorway. The song of the pines, her smiling eyes, my dad's room, and everything in it made me feel alive! Without speaking we walked back into the kitchen.

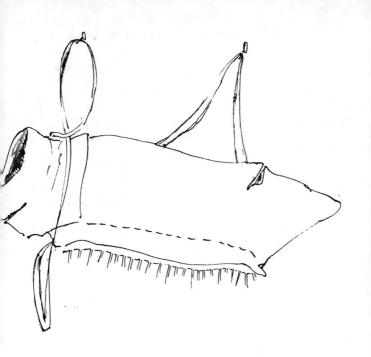

The savory smell of red beans
simmering on the cookstove and
cornbread steaming in its pan
caused me to wonder what else we
would have for supper—maybe a
platter of fried, crusty chicken or
juicy round steak. Just as I was
hoping we would eat, I heard
Agidutsi cleaning his boots on the

back steps. Agilisi held the door open as he entered, carrying in each hand a bucket of foaming cow's milk. Handing one to me and setting the other on a small wooden table by the keroscne cookstove, Agidutsi motioned toward four large crockery bowls and a shiny metal strainer. Setting my bucket on the corner of the table, I pushed down its wire handle, then with my right hand took a firm hold of the bucket's rim. With my left, I held the funnel-like milk strainer above the first of the thick crocks. Lifting the bucket, I poured the warm, white milk slowly through the fine-meshed screen until it came within two inches of the top of the bowl. Moving to the second bowl, I emptied the first bucket and set it on the floor under the table. The strainer was half-filled with white bubbly foam that crackled as each tiny bubble burst. I repeated the process with the second bucket, then set it down alongside the other. By morning both bowls would be covered with thick layers of rich cream. Satisfied with my performance, I turned with pretended indifference just in time to see Agidutsi's smile of approval.

I followed him outside to a full bucket of water resting on a soap-stained shelf nailed to the back wall of the house. Beside it rested a white porcelain wash pan and a new bar of Ivory soap. From a nail on the wall hung a faded but clean red towel.

Agidutsi poured the basin half-full and quickly scrubbed both hands, making plenty of lather as the soap bar slipped between his palms. Before washing his face, he poured out the used water, carefully rinsed away the scum from the sides, and refilled the bowl with fresh water. Finished, he lifted the towel from the nail and slowly dried first his face and neck, then his strong hands. I was fascinated by them; and as he poured out the second water and rinsed the pan, I stood there marveling at their apparent strength. I looked at mine, then washed as quickly as I could, avoiding the soap, and hurried in to supper.

Seeing the table both surprised and disappointed me. There was no fried chicken, fried steak, or any meat at all—just a huge bowl of red beans with pieces of salt pork floating on the steaming surface, two plates of thick cornbread, a bar of freshly churned butter glistening with tiny droplets of moisture, and a plate of sliced white onions. But I was so hungry that even without meat, supper looked delicious. As I stood waiting for my grandparents to be seated, I noticed the fourth place. I thought, "Company for supper with nothing but beans and cornbread?"

Just then an old Indian stepped through the kitchen doorway. He moved with the spirit and pride of a warrior, yet with the dignity and character of a statesman. As he sat in his place at the head of the table, his narrow, dark eyes observed me completely in a single, perceptive glance. Something about his unique presence spurred my recall of Dad's description of this venerable old man: ". . . the patience of the spider, the strength of the panther, and the wisdom of the great horned owl." These qualities had merged with perfect balance to mold the essence of this aged man. He was Redthrush, my great-grandfather.

Redthrush taught me the things I longed to know about my people. I learned that they had a place of refuge called Echota. In the days that followed, Pine Tree became my Echota. There within the quiet refuge of the pines, I listened and learned as never before. It was as if time were standing still, so that at last I could begin to understand who I was as a Tsalagi. Each morning Redthrush would awake before sunrise and slip quietly across the wooden floors to the front porch. Something within my sleeping mind would hear the soft thump of the screened door as it closed behind him, and within five minutes I would be dressed and sitting silently beside him.

Soon the morning would brighten, and I could see the gentle path Redthrush had worn through the pines. Just before the sun lifted

his face to greet the dawn,
Redthrush again would walk
toward the East. There he knelt
beside a shallow "branch" and
lifted his face to receive the soft
rays of courage beaming through
the tall pines. Then he would
stretch forth his hands and begin to
pray in Tsalagi. He often sang after
prayer, but he always sat for what
seemed to be an hour listening to
the song of Long Man, the Spirit of
the Provider.

Redthrush taught me to hear His
voice in the sound of running water
and in the whisper of the pines. It
was the same song that had
christened the small rocks beneath
the flow of my reinless river, and I
yearned to do more than just listen.
I wanted to understand.

As the days passed, the song of
Long Man taught me to hear the
words within my own heart. At
first, I heard only the rumble of
pride and anger. Then one night as I
lay on my cot listening to Agilisi
humming a Tsalagi tune, I recalled
her words, "This room and
everything in it—and now it is
yours." I was surrounded by my

dad. He too had stretched out on that very cot and no doubt had listened to Agilisi sing those same words:

*oo ne hla nuh hi oo we ji
i ga goo yuh he i
hna gwo jo suh wi oo lo se
i ga goo yuh ho nuh.*

My heart spoke of love, and I realized that a real home was more important to me than anything else.

Visualizing Agilisi's beauty as she hummed in the kitchen, I smiled. At last I had a home. Warm tears of joy and relief leaned forward from the corners of my eyes and kissed my cheeks. I was no longer alone.

Sleep came gently that night. For the first time since Dad had left, I laid aside my apprehension and trusted the invitation to slumber. The moon was still low in the sky when I first heard Aunt Liz: "Tobias, wipe your feet before you come in my house!" Then I saw myself standing there on her big white porch. The summer had ended, and once again time had sentenced me to the loneliness of the farm. "I hate it! I hate it! I will not stay! Do you hear me, Aunt Liz?" I shouted. "I will not stay!" Suddenly all the anger within me surfaced, and I drew back my arm and sailed my small canvas bag right through the glass in her fancy French door. Hearing the tinkling of falling glass, I threw open my eyes and sighed as I relaxed my legs and then my shoulders. Finally, I opened my fists.

I lay awake and ached at the thought of ever leaving my grandparents. I knew that as my legal guardians, Aunt Liz and Uncle Jim expected me to leave Pine Tree before the end of my summer vacation. Again and again I silently questioned, Why? Why should I return to loneliness and pain? It wasn't fair! Then, somewhere in between the why's, I forgot the question. The stars had walked across the summer sky, and I was tired. I felt myself drifting, drifting. Finally I let go and slept, only to be awakened by thin rays of sunshine that pierced my screened room and danced across my face. The sun had risen without me.

I reached for my T-shirt and jeans and then my socks and boots. I had not heard Redthrush and had missed our morning prayer. I heard Agilisi in the kitchen and smelled the sausage and coffee she and Agidutsi had had for breakfast. I walked bashfully through the door, asking to be excused from my morning meal so that I could walk through the pines. Agilisi smiled as if she understood my embarrassment and then nodded, "Walk toward the East."

Stepping in cadence to the distant popping of pump engines, I saw thin, bright rays of light stream through the pine thicket, emphasizing the quiet assurance of the breeze fluttering gently through the stately trees. From the pointing arms of this waking forest, hard young burrs grew beside dry and seasoned cones. Beneath the pines, the bright reflection of the early sun glistened on the surface of the quiet "branch."

Stilled by the strength and courage evident in the colorful

reflection of the morning sun, I silently admitted that no human hand or chance evolution could be the Master and Creator of this natural beauty. Momentarily secured and calmed, I became entranced by this mirrored scene. The watery canvas reflected the liquid blue of the East Texas sky hanging quietly beneath the rippling forms of giant pines. All this bathed in the radiant beauty spread by the light of the early morning sun! A gentle splash quietly disturbed the water's surface. The expanding radius formed by delicate ripples visualized the broad effect of a tiny pebble, and I knew that someone was near. When I looked across the water, my vision blurred as I saw that special someone, Redthrush.

Standing no more than seven yards away on the opposite bank of this shallow branch, he motioned me over. For nearly half an hour, we sat in silence under the stately branches of a towering slash pine. I knew that home would be wherever the two of us walked together. So certain that no tomorrow could

draw us closer, I revealed my determination to remain in Pine Tree. "Grandfather, I once was a wandering orphan who searched for love and acceptance. At last I have found my home and family. I am my father's son, and I belong here with his people. Life on the farm with Uncle Jim and Aunt Liz is like swimming upstream against the swiftness of the river, while here I am accepted and loved for myself. And so I have decided never to return to the loneliness of the farm."

To my dismay the three folds of Redthrush's forehead deepened; and without forfeit of their gentle love and compassion, his piercing eyes met mine with obvious disapproval. Placing his strong and confident hand on my shoulder, he said to me, "My son, it is not easy to leave behind those you love, especially to return to a lonely and cold path. Lonely because you choose to travel it with no one but yourself, and cold because you wear no blanket of love and happiness. Your path, my son, widens with each mile, for running is the easiest way to survive. In your heart you carry the burning arrows of bitterness and self-pity. These are weapons of destruction, not for others, but for yourself.

"Under these pines you have walked beside truth and beauty, and most important, you have given your heart the freedom to love. Because you have discovered and chosen the rich happiness of life in place of empty existence, you must also learn to swim the river of tears. I have told you that nothing is impossible because you are Tsalagi." Never before had his voice revealed the restraint of emotion.

Then Redthrush lifted his gaze to greet the East. As if mentally a part of something far beyond the sovereign beauty of the majestic pine forest, he stared through the shadowy depths. I watched, puzzled, as he softly voiced his thoughts in Tsalagi and then nodded as if in agreement. "Regardless of circumstances, our people have never run in fear. And so, my son, your determination is good, but your fears are unworthy of a Tsalagi. You must journey with me to the Qualla Boundary and there capture the ancient truths of our people, for only through their light can you discover the beauty of the white quiver."

Then he gently pulled my face to his strong shoulder and whispered, "My son, tomorrow we go home."

The anticipation of walking with Redthrush beneath the same seasoned trees which had befriended our ancestors erased any doubt that such an improbable dream could become reality. My grandmother had spent much of the night preparing food for our trip, and from within the white oak strips of the hand-woven basket escaped a combination of savory aromas that tempted my appetite. Yet not even this could halt the swaying of my heart in the warm breeze of my emotions as I stood on the third step within the doorway of the eastbound bus.

Fighting the tears of farewell and at the same time the eager joy of departure, I turned and waved to Agilisi and Agidutsi. They smiled reassuringly, their eyes expressing the truth of their love. And so, embraced by their warm smiles, I stepped forward and handed my ticket to the friendly driver. He chuckled as he caught sight of the heavy basket swinging from my right hand.

Most of the other passengers had boarded, and Redthrush nudged me on toward two vacant seats near the end of the bus. As I made my way down the center aisle, pairs of indignant eyes flashed first at us and then back and forth between each other. Silence resounded with the discipline of forced tolerance. I knew that this quiet indignation was the civilized way of reminding us of our place. I wanted to spit on everything that even hinted at being white. But my unspoken respect for the presence of Redthrush tempered my anger, for his wisdom and sensitivity and love distinguished him from ordinary men and lifted him to a plateau occupied only by the most renowned of sages.

Yet it seemed to me that the narrow minds of those passengers failed to grasp his greatness. To them, Redthrush was only a curious stranger belonging to a culture inferior to theirs.

Sitting next to the window, I stared into the red of the sandy hills as I struggled to ignore hostility surrounding two Indians on an all-white bus. Yet Redthrush smiled as if he were a part of a distant horizon, far beyond the shallow and stagnant ponds of hatred and social indignation. In the presence of his greatness my bitterness retreated behind my pride in being the great-grandson of Redthrush.

Unaware of a sleeping bitterness, I smiled as the sun crossed the morning sky and scaled its summit. The miles fled as vast fields of wilted cotton and drooping peanut stalks surrendered to thick forests and rolling hills. Soon the softness of waving ferns and poised vines gentled the aggressive strength of the towering pines. I stared into the ascending beauty of this unfamiliar terrain and listened as Redthrush began to speak softly to himself in Tsalagi.

With painstaking effort he completed the miniature white oak rabbit that he had been carving since we left Pine Tree. Gently blowing the dust from the small sanded figure, he proudly set the legendary trickster on his knee. Crooked stick in his paw, the clever little animal sat with cocky grin as if he were actually conjuring magic in the scorched pot at his feet.

Chuckling at the little creature, Redthrush's Southern accent uniquely emphasized words and phrases of significant meaning. With obvious delight he recounted the mischievous adventures of the infamous Tsistu, our people's legendary rabbit of trickery. According to Redthrush, Tsistu stole the other animals' water and then, ironically, through his own defiance was caught by the ingenious Tar Wolf. Later Tsistu lost his own prized tail after stealing Otter's soft and beautiful coat. It was Tsistu, the jealous, who conspired with Cricket to shear away Possum's beautiful tail; and finally Tsistu outsmarted himself and lost the race with Turtle. Redthrush must have told me hundreds of these stories as the miles hurried us closer to the mountains of our ancestors.

As he carved the graceful deer and bearded turkey, he explained that after Deer had been awarded his stately antlers and Turkey had stolen his beard from Turtle, nature had patterned their descendants with these same characteristics. Through all Redthrush's accounts of birds and animals, he illustrated how virtues such as honesty and courage or weaknesses such as jealousy and selfishness had resulted in the distinct markings of each bird and animal.

Drawing from his own experience and wisdom, he theorized that the lines on a man's face reveal his truest nature, and that each of us as individuals pass on the most valuable or wicked results of our innermost strengths and weaknesses. According to Redthrush, love is the fertile soil for

all virtues, and selfishness the stagnant breeding pond of all evils. He told me that our people believed that evil is the result of man's selfish discord with nature and that before selfishness flourished as the choking weed of this world, our people and all of life were happy. His words hinted at a truth I longed to understand.

Redthrush explained that within the mountains of our ancestors grows the flower called the Indian Pipe, and that before the blooming of this small flower, our people had their first quarrel with another Indian nation. It seems that for months the stubborn chiefs sat in council discussing the war. As they solemnly smoked their divining tobacco, our Provider lost patience with their lack of sincere effort toward attaining peace. And so He turned the old chiefs into the first cluster of Indian Pipe flowers to serve as a warning to all men that their rituals and tobacco should be for peace. Then as final reminder to our people, He hung great clouds of blue smoke above our heads to remain always until there is peace among all men. "My son," he said to me, "the smoky haze of our mountains has long since hovered as a reminder to the Tsalagï to strive forever for peace."

Time, however, soon taught that such peace for me would continue to be elusive. Although my dream of walking the hills of our ancestors had come true, bitterness and hatred soon awakened and turned life into a nightmarish reality.

Reaching down with confidence to caress the land and rivers that passed between two sunrises and sunsets, the sky herself had never altered her clear and blue or midnight and starry countenances. Yet in the wakening red of the third morning, she gracefully christened the sovereign beauty of our ancestral mountains with a delicately translucent and smoky blue. Alerted to the reality that for centuries the Tsalagi had gazed into that same hovering blue, I pulsed with an eagerness to become more than a spectator, in essence to become a living part of those mountains and their majestic beauty.

The Oconaluftee River escaped the heights and roared melodically between hidden coves and sheer slabs of stone. Rushing over the stoic red boulders wedged solidly in the river's natural mosaic bed, the water's surge backlashed into foamy white waves. Beyond its tortuous and swift trail rose the deep emerald splendor of mountain forests.

The sun's light clung to the swaying white fingers of the sourwood bloom and flickered from leaf to leaf as if reflected by thousands of small mirrors. Pine and oak, balsam and poplar, maple and spruce, all stood erect, united, and at peace with life in their native soil.

The commanding beauty and quiet reverence of those stately mountains voiced an ancestral welcome which silently met some innate need hidden within the depths of my emotions. Surveying the grandeur of our Smokies, I began to understand the complexity of those compelling words, "My son, tomorrow we go home."

At last our bus screeched to a halt

in the little town of Cherokee, North Carolina, set in the foothills of the Great Smokies. The other passengers scrambled past us with cameras and sunglasses to join the throng of tourists already crowding the streets. Redthrush and I slowly descended the steps to the pavement below. Suddenly we were misfits no longer. Those same eyes which had once condescended now sparkled with curiosity. We were "real live Indians."

We had not changed. Yet there in new surroundings, we no longer were intruders of another world. We stood upon *our* land and among *our* people. We belonged. Redthrush ignored the tourists' requests to take his picture; I detected that he was almost annoyed.

While I waited for the bus driver to unload our baggage, Redthrush greeted a young man dressed in jeans and a plaid shirt who wore his straight, black, shoulder-length hair parted in the middle. I watched as he and Redthrush embraced affectionately. Timidly I wondered, "Who can this guy be?" For some reason I had not expected to meet more of Dad's family.

Joe and I became best friends. He was my third cousin and two years older, but we really understood each other. His family lived just up the mountain from Redthrush's cabin. We ate most of our meals with them.

That first afternoon in Cherokee was like a great family reunion. We dined on fried squirrel and tasty bean bread with baked apples for dessert. As we ate, Redthrush and his children laughingly reminisced about the past. Then as the sun slipped into the mountain's blue haze, we said good night and walked across the cove to Redthrush's small cabin.

The simple structure of chinked logs and red clay depicted the strength and character of more than an era. It had been built over a hundred years before by Redthrush's grandfather, a man who had hidden in caves rather than submit to a forced removal from the mountains of his fathers. Inside his cabin he had built a huge fireplace for his small family. That same fireplace surrounded by aged timbers continued to warm the chilly night air in the cabin that belonged now to Redthrush.

I sat beside Redthrush listening to the sounds of the night and watching the dancing flames consume the oak logs. What a memorable evening! I still can see him sitting there whittling a small raccoon from a piece of wild cherry as his tall-backed rocker slowly squeaked back and forth across the smooth plank floor. Occasionally a smile revealed his subtle humor, as his twinkling eyes concealed some secret just waiting for the proper moment to be heard. I delighted in this unique characteristic because it made me forget myself and laugh.

That same humor had kept Redthrush young. In spite of his white hair and dark weathered skin, his eyes were happy and alert. They had watched the passing of almost a century and had seen much more than the eyes of an ordinary man; they had pierced all surface meanings and searched for truth. Deep folds marked his low forehead and numbered the years he had spent in concentrated "knowing." Time, however, had failed to wither the flowers of youth within him. Redthrush remained the gift of springtime.

The warm air filled our one-room cabin as Redthrush completed the small creature, skillfully using even the natural grain of the wood to enhance each detail. These carvings provided his livelihood and were in great demand. Once each week I carried his delicately carved masterpieces to the co-op, known to tourists as the Qualla Arts and Crafts Center. The small stone building housed the work of the Eastern Cherokee.

Redthrush displayed his work there alone because it was solely owned and operated by "the people" themselves. He loved his people, and as one day followed another that summer in Cherokee, I began to love them too. Warm and gentle by nature, they were bound by more than a common ancestry. Pride in themselves and in their past had woven them into a blanket of hope for the future. As I watched and listened, I longed to become a single thread in that beautiful blanket.

My first chance came when I accepted an offer to usher at the outdoor drama "Unto These Hills." Five nights a week, dressed as a Tsalagi, I directed tourists to their seats in the amphitheater. There they watched the spectacular story of the Cherokee nation unfold. On the first night of my new job, I was warm and friendly to these visitors, but as I myself witnessed the drama and heard the tragic circumstances that had gripped our people years before, my old resentment and bitterness returned. It seemed as if each time I heard the story retold, my heart wept. More than once on that first night, I had to fight back warm tears.

There were moments when the spectators seemed stunned by the injustices which had stripped the Cherokee people of their land, their freedom, and their joy. Yet, more often they laughed, or so it seemed to me. My taut throat ached with restraint each night as the dramatic scenes drew to an end. The closing scene showed the Tsalagi families faced with insurmountable loss, leaving for "the Arkansas." Just outside the gates of the stockade in which they had been confined, they lifted their hearts in song:

oo ne hla nuh hi oo we ji
i ga goo yuh he i
hna gwo jo suh wi oo lo se
i ga goo yuh ho nuh.

Then, bowing their heads, they listened to the prayer of their minister as he stood before them, arms outstretched, pleading to the Provider:

Gadusi widigagani nahna juhdidalehuhyaga agwalinigohiyadiyagi oonelanuhhi agiyadeliyagi nayagi oowoenuhhi galuhladi ale suhlohi.

With each performance those words spoke more pleadingly to my own spirit.

Then came the clear voice of the narrator as he repeated those closing words in English: "I will lift up my eyes to the hills. From whence does my help come? My help comes from the Lord, who made heaven and earth." Those were the words of the Psalm that hung upon the wall of Agilisi's kitchen. Yet my cousin Joe told me that because of these same words, Redthrush had repeatedly refused the revered role of the minister in the "Unto These Hills" pageant.

One Sunday morning as Redthrush and I sat watching the sun awaken the mountains, I pondered his stubborn refusal to accept the coveted honor because of the prayer so special to our people. Were the words contrary to our traditional religious beliefs? As usual, the perceptive Redthrush recognized my puzzlement. Finally he questioned, "What troubles you, my son?" I knew that his question gave me permission to ask. Only after several minutes did his answer come.

"My son," he began, "from the first days our people have worshipped the Creator. According to ancient beliefs, He exists in the form of three beings known to our people as 'Cho ta auh ne le eh,' the Elder Fires Above. Yet, long ago our people adopted the Christian faith. As a child I went to church where our own ministers spoke to us about Jesus Christ, the Christian God of love. I listened and believed. Then as a young man I began to look at the plight of the Indian nations and soon questioned a religion where men allowed greed and dishonesty to govern their actions. I compared Christianity to our ancient religion, and decided that I could not continue to accept a religion which speaks of love but acts with greed.

"My God is the Provider. He created everything beautiful and good. Beauty can only be created through love. And so, my son, you see the Creator is the true God of love. No god, not even the power of death, can overcome Him.

"Christianity speaks of the triumph of life over death; and yet Christians brought us smallpox, burned our towns, and sold our people into slavery."

Redthrush paused and gazed toward the East as if to find the answer to a puzzle within his thoughts. After several long minutes of silence, he turned to me and explained, "My son, I have known Christians like Will Thomas who with kindness and generosity befriended our people. For many years I have pondered the contrast between their love and peace and the death and destruction which walked behind their brothers. The one basic difference I have found in those few is the absence of selfishness. Perhaps, then, the power of death is not Jesus, but rather selfishness itself.

"Our people have traditionally believed that through man's selfish discord with nature, evil entered our world. I have learned that evil hides behind lies and excuses. Perhaps man has often worn the Christian mask as a disguise, fooling men into believing that their actions were justified.

"I must learn the answer to this question. I must know if the Christian's God, Jesus, and the Creator are the same. Someday Long Man, the Spirit of our Provider, will carry my prayer to the Holy Mountain and return with an answer. Until then I will walk in peace and happiness.

"But your search, my son, must begin within your own spirit. You must call upon the Provider to remake you and grant you the beauty of *do tsu wa*, the redbird.

"Within your spirit, my son, grow seeds of destruction. Someday they will choke freedom and beauty from your life and leave you the emptiness of existence. The choice is yours. Will you seek revenge or *ado dhlvhi so? di yi?*"

I had listened to his words, yet did not understand. Silently I questioned, "What is the meaning of this *ado dhlvhi so? di yi?*"

Once again the perceptive Redthrush knew my thoughts. He answered, "The idea of remaking yourself is complex and yet simple. It is a spiritual journey that a man's mind and heart must make. Together they must walk the circle of life until each decides to leave behind the burdens which delay their journey. The mind must choose to 'know' rather than 'think,' just as the heart must seek love and peace rather than revenge and anger. Only then can the

Provider begin to change us so that others see within us the beauty of *do tsu wa*."

I longed for that beauty, and according to Redthrush my heart had taken the very first steps toward *ado dhlvhi so? di yi*. He believed that someday I would find the answers to my question and discover peace and its shadow, happiness.

The sun had reached its highest place in the sky, and Redthrush had answered my questions. But more importantly he gave me my Tsalagi name, "Do tsu wa."

Tobias would stay behind while Do tsu wa searched for peace and happiness.

As Do tsu wa, my spirit belonged to the mountains of my ancestors as instinctively as the wild strawberry and flowering dogwood. As the days passed, this intuitive kinship for the Qualla Boundary and our people blossomed into a fragrant flower with delicate petals of security and happiness. And yet there I learned the painful lesson that no people or place could fill the emptiness within me.

My rendezvous with this truth began one morning toward the end of the summer. I stood in the doorway of Redthrush's small cabin and watched two small boys amble by, laughing and swinging their cane poles. I stared at them with amazement, for I could not accept that an Indian and a white would walk so openly as close friends.

Remaining at a conservative distance, I followed the curious two until they reached a small pond fed by the Raven Fork. They sat contentedly, cooling their bare feet in the clear water, then shared a sandwich and drank from the same thermos. Two boys from different races sat in each other's confidence, sharing and laughing together. I sighed in relief, for below the hazy blue of these ancient mountains, children seemed free to play with each other regardless of color or language.

Satisfied, I strolled away from the two young fishermen and followed the damp and soft path of ground pine until my attention shifted to the swift water racing down and through the dense undergrowth of rhododendron and pepper bush. Above me lay Mingo Falls. Fascinated by the determined surge, I climbed steadily upward, tracing the sound of running water. After several hundred rugged feet and beyond a slippery boulder, a narrow path inched its precarious way through oak and poplar. To avoid sliding, I clung to sturdy branches and vine-covered bushes and struggled up the steep, rocky trail. Some 700 feet up the mountain a huge pitch pine lay suspended as a natural bridge above a gurgling stream and reached defiantly across a wide ravine to the opposite side.

At the three-foot base of the natural bridge, I stood motionless and silent, listening to the forceful roar of falling water. Scrambling agilely across the rough pine until I stood above the middle of the ravine, I stared upward into the noble face of Mingo Falls. Three hundred feet above me the cold, thundering water poured in four sparkling cascades down a solid stone wall, only to rise again in mist as it pounded and smoothed the rocks below. The grandeur of the surging falls against a tiered staircase of solid mountain seemed to echo a welcome from my ancestors.

Crossing to the right of the shadowy ravine, I waded precariously through the frigid water and over the slippery boulders until I reached the same narrow trail which had inched its way up the rugged mountainside. The rocky path gradually became steeper until its sharp angle forced me to crawl and pull myself toward the red maple and fir balsam shading the crested height. The agony and pain of aching muscles and bruised hands and knees shouted a cry of fatigue and surrender, but the spirit of youthful defiance pushed on until at last, out of breath and exhausted, I stood triumphantly on the mountain's lofty top. Proudly lifting my outstretched and weary arms to greet the subtle blue of the Smokies, I trembled with joy and excitement; for in spite of my mixed blood, I had become an irrevocable part of my ancestors' mountains and had discovered the ultimate meaning for the ambiguous word, home.

The mountains of our forefathers swept me tenderly into their infinite embrace and silently whispered the radiant acceptance and eternal reassurance that no human voice can communicate. The boundless beauty of twinkling forests set against the hazy horizon of rising peaks joined hands with the delicate strength of sleepy coves waking to the hush of swift mountain waters. Together they created a fourth dimension in which time could bear no consequence. The ancient Spirit of those mountains resounded in a vivid beauty which touched my every sense. Hidden within their majesty lay more than acceptance and identity. Redthrush had said that I must walk among all men as the dauntless red fox who through wisdom remains free and untamed. That wisdom rested in the tranquil strength and omniscient Spirit of these mountains.

Quiet beside that crested brink of christening water, I gazed in awe at the vastness of those peaks and the intricacy of their life. Each stately pine and towering spruce stood on tiptoe reaching upward to distant summits that rose majestically above the smoky blue. I stared into their shadowy depths and wondered if they, too, were relinquishing the grief and injustice they had seen, in hope of that legendary promise of peace for all men. No cathedral or tabernacle has ever equaled the reverent beauty and serenity of that mountain sanctuary. Once again I silently admitted that no human hand or chance evolution could be the Creator of nature's unparalleled splendor, painted with strength and patience on the delicate canvas of time.

Somewhere within the span of that timeless and spiritual dimension dwelt the illusive Truth essential for my strength and survival in a world of bias and conflict. I needed more than a people and home, and the simple dignity and rare beauty of each. My journey had triumphed in its search for both, yet still I yearned for something. Truth had shattered my insecurity as an Indian and had replaced it with pride as a Tsalagi. I had dismounted my lame and weary horse and could stand tall before myself and all other men. Yet smothered beneath the damp leaves of uncertainty and emptiness, the coals within me still smoldered. In the glare of that depressing reality, my eyes left the promising horizon and cast their somber reflection to the fragile Indian Pipe growing wild beside the surging stream.

I stared bewildered at the waxy white of that small cluster of flowers and pondered the truth captured within the legend of their origin. With their tiny heads bowed under the strain of a long and difficult council for peace, each saddened face frowned wearily in despair as if saying, "There is no hope for peace among men."

Considering these despairing words, I searched the tranquil expanse of our ancestral mountains for Wisdom and Truth. According to legend, the smoke draped across those gentle peaks would hover above until all men learned to live together in peace. Redthrush had said that our Provider did not intend for men to fear each other. Such fear, he had said, breeds injustice and violence with the same cruelty that once ravaged these beautiful mountains, severing 18,000 Tsalagi from their loved ones and homes.

And yet, more than a century later, two young fishermen were sitting contentedly side by side, laughing as if their forefathers had never mistrusted or hated one another. I wondered if their generation would become sprouting buds, to awaken an insensitive world to love and inspire peace among all men. But my ingrained suspicions could not accept such hope without skepticism. The wise Redthrush must have perceived the intensity of my bitterness and the urgency of *ado dhlvhi so? di yi* when he had said, "Do tsu wa, to find peace and its shadow, happiness, you must remake yourself." He had brought me home so that I could discover the requisite truth cached within the beauty of the white quiver, and then remake myself with the radiant spirit of the same truth.

There on the mountain's soft ground pine I knelt and recalled the quiver's distinct beauty. Seven smooth and flawless seams, stitched with seasoned and taut sinew, bound the staunch leather of that aged quiver. Stiffened through age, the leather stood upright with independence and pride, and yet time had not sallowed the purity of the doe's fine white hair.

But why was the quiver empty, and why had I scaled the summit only to meet defeat in my victory? The old doubts and queries flickered and then defiantly flamed to defend the failure of my quest and silence the echo of my unhappiness.

In my anger I stood with clenched fists and demanded God's answers. "Why?" I shouted. "Why?" Finally, not listening, not caring, I stomped the fragile Indian Pipe. Tobias had overtaken Do tsu wa, and the journey for *ado dhlvhi so? di yi* was delayed.

PART TWO

Where Shall I Find Help?

The hum of honeybees erased that vivid memory of my fourteenth summer and unfolded a tangible, living world where beauty had matured and mellowed. The river breeze, crisp and light with freshness, brightened the morning with the symphony of a hundred vibrant songs.

Stretched out on my familiar cottonwood, I wakened to the harmony of nature and the reality of my own freedom. For seven long years, confined behind steel and concrete, I had longed to be free. I found it difficult to believe that the governor had signed my release. Leaning down to splash my face with the cool, refreshing water, I quietly drank in the serene beauty resting calmly upon the mirrored surface. A tiny drone floated within the reflection of the morning red as if he, too, had come to face the East and pray in view of the rising sun.

Embraced by the dawn, I leaned

against the rough bark of my old cottonwood and once again communed with the Provider. My prayer rose not as a petition for strength and courage, but instead ascended in appreciation for another chance at life. The farm and its bottomland belonged to me now. Aunt Liz had been dead for five years and Uncle Jim for two. In spite of the pain I had brought to both of them, they had left everything to me. Perhaps I had been wrong about their love.

Life seemed ironic, twisting and turning in events that never should have happened. I wondered how many like me had been branded as misfits, when in reality we were merely the victims of circumstances—some, to be sure, of our own making.

There on my cottonwood I thought about the years of hatred which had narrowed my vision and blurred my reasoning. Redthrush had recognized my growing bitterness and year after year had cautioned me about my anger and hostility. During memorable summers on the Boundary, I had tried desperately to change. Time and again I had climbed Mingo Falls in search of *ado dhlvhi so? di yi* only to meet defeat in my victory over the mountain.

My heart and mind became bound by their burdens; and so by the time I entered college, I had become the prisoner of my own anger and bitterness. As their slave, I experienced no real happiness. I longed to be Do tsu wa and walk within his beauty. Again and again I heard the words of Redthrush, "Do tsu wa, to find peace and its shadow, happiness, you must remake yourself." Because I had failed to experience *ado dhlvhi so? di yi* atop Mingo Falls, I sought to remake myself through the spiritual experience of drugs. But even their world of visions offered me no freedom, and again I awoke to the harsh reality of Tobias.

Eventually I blamed society for the bitterness and anger which bound me. My cousin Joe agreed, and together we became militants seeking an end to the political and social injustice which history had recorded against the Indian nations.

I really believed that at last I had become a thread in that blanket of hope.

Redthrush understood our anguish, but steadfastly disagreed with our tactics. We sought the wisdom of his counsel and his prayers, but rejected his admonition that the hope of our people lay in a spiritual victory. Redthrush revered the principles of democracy and reminded us of the proud history of our people.

I had not forgotten their accomplishments: the Sequoyan "alphabet," a national newspaper, a written constitution, and a democratic form of government. Years after the forced removal of the entire Cherokee nation from the land of their fathers, those of our people who had hidden in the mountains managed to buy back their land, rebuild their homes, and reorganize their government. Working together, they restored the beauty of their nation. Again the phoenix had risen from its ashes. "But why?" I had questioned Redthrush, "why the ashes?"

Gazing toward the East, he lifted

his right hand and pointed to the smoky haze resting above the mountains of our people. "Our Creator," he said, "hung smoke above these mountains to remind us of the evil within selfishness. You, my son, seek to change this evil; and yet, I tell you that you carry it within yourself. Only when you and men of all colors learn to remake yourselves will selfishness leave this world."

I believed Redthrush, but refused to change. Anger and hostility continued to plot my fate until one night in a bar, filled with alcohol and rage, I choked a drunken fool until his lips would never again belittle another with the phrase "half-breed." Only animals breed; men bear sons and daughters. Yet men also control their emotions; I had not. For my crime, a crime that I had abhorred in history, I was charged, convicted, and sentenced.

Redthrush had often spoken of the danger of my bitterness. Even though I had sought *ado dhlvhi so? di yi*, at the same time, I had struggled for the right of revenge. I had tested the wisdom of the ages and had lost. Seven years in a small concrete room had taught me to hear truth where once I had only listened. I sighed in relief that I had been pardoned. The Provider had granted me another chance to become Do tsu wa.

Gazing at the still and brilliant reflection of the rising sun, I watched my image disappear within the mirrored splendor of morning light. Gradually I began to grasp the essence of *ado dhlvhi so? di yi*. Perhaps, at last, I could "remake" myself.

At rest against the strongest limb of my cottonwood, I again pondered the union of the native pecan and water elm into one solid timber. As I searched beyond the depths of its fraternal branches, the morning light gently erased their shadows and danced across seven golden lobes of honey. The unmarred beauty of the succulent span masked the ugly scar which lay beneath as blatant evidence of the agony experienced by the two specied trees.

In disbelief I scrambled the

hardwood distance to the bank, and there stared in wonder at that magnificent honeycomb glistening with simplicity and revelation. I marveled at the daring defiance of a hive of bees that would build on a torn, gnarled scar rather than within the protective shelter of a hollow. Yet no animal had ravaged the defenseless combs for their sweet nectar.

I chuckled as I recalled that fateful summer day when, climbing that same freakish tree, I had anticipated a cavern of golden honey only to be disappointed by the bitter taste of raw sap. As I pondered the transfiguration of that gnarled scar and its bitter sap into a beautiful honeycomb, something stirred in the depths of my emotions. Gazing up through the warm tears of a small boy, I smiled and thanked the bees for the most meaningful welcome ever. The Provider had created a unique tribute to nature's counterpart, time. The rare beauty of that simple honeycomb unveiled the climactic truth that for everything there is a purpose. God had mysteriously chosen the gnarled knothole as the site of creation, and in so doing had hidden the ugly scar beneath the beauty of life.

The Creator had remade the gnarled scar, and all that remained was a natural work of art and phenomenal splendor. Once again truth had unfolded from a simple miracle inscribed with perception on still another of nature's edifying pages.

Down through the swaying branches drifted the redbird's enchanting whistle: "Do tsu! do tsu hwi!" As Do tsu wa I returned the small creature's gentle call. Together we shared a unique kinship.

A fox squirrel barked from a distant pecan and then chattered wildly as if to awaken any late sleepers. Reaching toward the waving treetops, I yawned, then ambled downriver toward the old river bridge. Hearing the rush of surging water ahead, I stared through the filtering light and into the smiling countenance of an infinite sky. Listening to the warm breeze as it sauntered through the heights of sycamore and pecan, I drifted with its quiet hush and considered the tranquility and rapture of the river bottom. Such was the peace and happiness that I had always longed to abide within me. Then from the crowded cache of my memory stepped the soft, yet firm counsel of Redthrush, "Do tsu wa, to find peace and its shadow, happiness, you must remake yourself."

Earlier that morning nature had taught me the essence of *ado dhlvhi so? di yi*. My journey in search of a new self had begun, yet still I wandered. I had learned from my past mistakes and now had chosen to carry the empty white quiver rather than to wear the red feather of war. Calmed by the sound of running water, I considered the danger of ideals and their fragile hopes. Nature had created and protected the simple beauty of the defenseless honeycomb; but who, I asked, would protect me from the anger of old wounds and the ugliness of their scars?

Across the river's quiet flow drifted the dove's assuasive call, "Gu le! gu le! gu le!" I smiled from within as *Gule disgo nihi* serenaded me with his melodic song; for in spite of the years transpired, the beauty and companionship of the river had not faded.

There among the trees and animals that I loved, I waited for Redthrush. His letter had read: "Do tsu wa, sit beside the sound of running water. Before the sun reaches its height in the sky, you will sense the presence of an old man and know that I am near."

The sun had almost climbed to her summit when a rare and beautiful silence quieted the bottomland. Peace seemed to whisper through the towering pecans, calming everything within her gentle touch. Then from behind me, the song of a small bird filled the morning air.

I sat motionless, listening to the flutter of wings and the approaching song. Each note brought the greeting closer. Finally I felt the gentle touch of springtime on my shoulder. Tears slowly made their way down my face as I heard, "Si yu, Do tsu wa." Turning, I greeted the dark, perceptive eyes of my beloved Redthrush. Once again I recalled Dad's words: "The patience of the spider, the strength of the panther, and the wisdom of the great horned owl." But something was missing and more than his silence convinced me that Redthrush was different.

First, a butterfly graced the air without his so much as noticing its beauty, then the dove called to his unlistening ears. Redthrush had changed. His face was thinner, his countenance tired. The cold wind of despair had broken his spirit, and fear now dominated his eyes.

As we sat listening to the flow of the ancient river, the warm air laughed with the songs of redbird, mockingbird, and bluebird. Three fox squirrels complained about the heat, while four others played chase from limb to limb. Yet Redthrush seemed not to notice their antics. Perhaps on this day he resented their laughter.

We sat in silence beneath the

towering pecan until finally Redthrush confessed, "My son, I have come that together we can fast and pray. Before I leave this world, I must gain the spiritual wisdom to know 'the way' for our people."

The rest of the afternoon passed without comment as the warm air stretched out and napped between the towering pecans. Even the squirrels seemed lazy. I watched as Redthrush prepared himself for ritual and prayer. I, too, sought answers and hoped that at last my heart and mind would lay aside their burdens and discover *ado dhlvhi so? di yi.*

As the sun settled against the horizon, Redthrush rose and walked to the water's edge. He knelt on the sloping bank and reached out to trap the cool water in his gnarled hands. Moistening his weathered lips, he drank, then stared into the quiet flow as if sensing some cache of truth within its depths. Moments later he stood, faced the East, and lifted his gaze above the towering pecans. Narrowing his eyes, he wrinkled his forehead and listened as if his search for truth had soared beyond the past or present. I watched in awe as his spirit attuned with some silent unknown.

Then above the gentle call of the mourning dove, Redthrush summoned me. "Do tsu wa, come. Journey with me beneath the sound of running water, for our Provider's Spirit speaks of new life."

Together we stepped onto the gravel, wading against the current before sinking beneath its swiftness. The water, cold and refreshing, gently swept us downstream. Before long I felt a kick in my ribs and realized that the aged Redthrush had surfaced past me.

Together we climbed the sandy bank. Redthrush seemed cold, and so I gathered twigs and three pieces of dry wood for fire. Side by side, we sat enjoying the warmth of the dancing flames and gazing silently into their glow. As the hour darkened, lightning bugs darted in and out of the shadows like small lanterns of truth. Even after years of watching them appear and disappear, I still pondered their source of energy. While Redthrush pensively sat humming a Tsalagi tune, the warmth of our fire cooled to coals. Lying beneath a tent of pecan branches, I looked into the face of a twinkling star, recalling the vision of my youth. My thoughts then drifted into dreams about Mom and Dad. Together we hurried through the stillness of night, only to bid farewell before the first rays of the morning sun.

Rising to greet the dawn, I saw Redthrush kneeling beside the running stream, in the tradition of our people. I, too, believed that the Provider sent rays of courage from His sun. The woods welcomed the morning with laughter and joy. The dove sang, and Do tsu wa darted across the river whistling a tune of freedom. A gentle breeze sighed through the leaves as if to join in nature's song of praise. But above it all the gentle christening of the river's flow seemed to lift the silent prayer of the aged Redthrush.

Returning to our simple camp and gazing toward the East, Redthrush smiled. He assured me that Long Man had heard his prayer and that the sound of running water had taken wing and carried his petition to the Provider. "Soon," he said, "his answer will come." So our fast continued.

Finally, during the second afternoon, hunger left me as quickly as it had come. The day had been long and hot, and thirst soon replaced hunger. Moving to the reinless river, I watched red dragonflies flit across my path. Nearing the water's edge, I saw a turtle look up from his sun nap, then plunge off the old sycamore only to disappear into the gentle stream. I waded waist deep into the river, scooped the cool water into my hands, and drank.

Hours passed before the sun painted a triumphant glow upon the suede of the horizon. Seeking an escape, I called for sleep. Yet again and again I would awaken with a throat and mouth "full of cotton" and go in the moon's path to the water's edge where again I would drink. Still thirst clung defiantly.

PART THREE

My Help Comes from God, Maker of Heaven and Earth

ith unquenched thirst, I greeted the morning of the third dawn as the sun rose from behind a stoic cottonwood across the river. As Long Man glided through the leaves above me, I listened to his song. Below me the sound of running water awakened the forest world as the rising sun brought an end to the long night. Yet as my heart smiled at being a part of such beauty, the piercing spears of brilliance intensified my giant of thirst.

Then I saw Redthrush rise from the motionless position he had maintained throughout the night and go to kneel beside the flowing waters. Facing the East, he slowly and reverently lifted his hands to the crystal heavens and petitioned the Provider. "Bend down your ear and give me answers," he pleaded, "for my days disappear like smoke. My health is broken and my heart is sick; it is trampled like grass and is withered. I have cried until tears no longer come; my heart is broken, my spirit poured out, as I see what is happening to my people. I weep for their hurt; I stand silent with grief."

Suddenly a great hush fell over us. Not even the sound of running water was heard above the breath of Long Man as he moved silently through the trees. With the swiftness of a summer storm, a blanket of heavy clouds covered the day.

Redthrush peered knowingly into the darkness and then moved to my side. His eyes shouted with expectation as if he sensed the presence of the Creator Himself. But I was frightened, for never had I witnessed such a hush or seen the sky appear so angry.

Instinctively, Redthrush broke the silence of my fears with the counsel of a prophet. "Do tsu wa!" he shouted in excitement. "Look, the Provider is all-powerful. He draws up the water which the skies pour down."

But I saw no rain, only huge ominous clouds, hovering darkness, and the shadows of its silence.

Then thunder rode the sky
descending from the East.

"Listen, Do tsu wa!" Redthrush
whispered. "Listen to the thunder
of His voice. It rolls across the
heavens. We cannot comprehend
the greatness of His power. For He
directs the snow, the showers, and
the storm to fall upon the earth.
From the south comes the rain,
from the north, the cold."

With each word his eyes seemed
to penetrate more deeply the dark
and hovering sky. Suddenly an even
greater hush fell around us,
silencing even the thunder. Then
without warning, a great bolt of fire
leaped from the heights of heaven
and struck the majestic cottonwood
towering just before us above the
other bank of the river. As it ripped
its way down, tearing the bark and
grounding itself in the roots below,
an explosion of light burst from the
heavens. Its radiance was so
blinding that Redthrush and I
covered our faces and fell to the
earth.

Lying there, faces down, we heard
these words, spoken as if from the
source of light itself: "You seek

answers for yourselves and your people? Then listen to me, for I am Wisdom. I existed before this earth began, before the oceans were created or the mountains and hills were made. Whoever finds me finds Truth and Life. As children you called on me. My name is Jesus."

At the very sound of that name everything within me screamed in defiance. Life had taught me that Jesus was a myth, a fantasy conjured up by men who needed a Savior. Common sense told me that the voice in the wind was just another Christian trick. Some "missionary" was trying to "save the souls of two misguided Indians."

Lifting my head I shouted, "I'm no fool!" But the piercing light forced me to cover my face again. Angry and determined, I refused to submit to this cruel hoax. Shouting into the wind, I exclaimed, "Whoever you are, go away. We don't need you or your god!"

Then as if to silence my angry words, the light intensified, engulfing me and forcing me back to the ground.

Every muscle within me tensed. Then above the pounding of my heart, I heard His resolute yet calm reply. "Listen to me! My words are those of my Father, the Holy One. He says this to you and your people: 'I am God, both in heaven and earth; there is no God other than Me! You must obey what I tell you today, so that all will be well with you and your children.'"

Redthrush had asked the Provider for an answer for our people. But, I questioned, can all this be real? Yet above my racing thoughts, His voice continued: "I don't want your offerings; I want your love; I want you to know me. Why do you look everywhere except to the Most High God? I tell you this, you will always be like a crooked bow that misses its targets until you do."

I thought, "If these words are really those of our Provider, then I am confused. What more could He expect from me? Each morning for seven years I have faced the East and prayed in the tradition of our people. I have set aside my revenge and have vowed to walk in peace among all men. What more can I do? And Redthrush, the most spiritual man I know, how can he be like a crooked bow? What more can a man do than remake himself?"

Then above my own thoughts, I heard Jesus explain: "I tell you this—you must be born spiritually. Men can only produce human life, but my Spirit gives new life from heaven. Just as you hear the wind but cannot tell where it will go next, so it is with the Spirit who leads into all Truth."

"But surely," I reasoned, "there must be more than one way, and Redthrush has asked for a way for the Indian people."

"I am the Way," He said. This time His voice was directly in front of me. I actually felt His presence, as if I could reach out and touch Him.

Standing there before me, He offered to quench my thirst.

"Are you thirsty?" He asked. "Then come to me and drink, and from your innermost being will flow rivers of Living Water."

The compassion in His voice assured me of His infinite love.

Jesus had died to buy us and was alive to remake us. My eyes filled with tears as I reached out to touch Him.

Just then His light intensified, then vanished. Thrusting open my eyes, I saw only dark clouds hovering above us. Suddenly they opened, and the rain came down in torrents. In less than a minute. Redthrush and I were soaked from head to toe. Then the morning sun broke through and showered us with love and warmth. The God above all gods had spoken.

The air smelled fresh and clean, and once again the river "bottom" began to sing. From across the river, *Gule disgo nihi* called to us, "Gu le, gu le."

Beside me knelt Redthrush. Tiny drops of water trickled from his long white hair onto his aged cheeks. His head bowed, his shoulders slumped, he mumbled something in Tsalagi and then nodded as if in agreement.

Slowly he reached out and placed his firm hand on my shoulder. I turned and helped him stand. Together we stepped closer to the sound of running water. We stood there silently listening to the song of Long Man. I knew then that He had always been more than just my friend. The sun had risen to a height just above the three cottonwoods on the other bank. The warmth of those smiling rays lifted the chill from my shivering form. Across the sky twin rainbows stretched from East to West with unparalleled beauty.

Turning to Redthrush, I beheld an even greater miracle. Winter had left, and spring had returned to his countenance. His eyes spoke clearly of a joy they had never known. My throat ached with emotion as I watched the morning light dance across the tears that flowed down his cheeks. His smiling eyes stared with assurance into the expanse of infinite blue. Stretching forth his arms to greet the East, he spoke slowly, reverently in Tsalagi, lifting his voice in prayer.

As I heard his gentle words, "I will lift up mine eyes unto the hills . . .," his prayer became mine. At last the heart and mind of Tobias

chose to "know" with love and peace rather than to "think" with anger and revenge. A gentle breeze touched my shoulder, and Long Man began to sing within me. As I heard His song, my thirst disappeared and I knew that I had been remade. The white quiver was no longer empty. Life had replaced existence. Do tsu wa was free.

That hour marked the beginning of a new day.